BOOK CURSES

BOOK
CURSES

ELEANOR BAKER

BODLEIAN
LIBRARY
PUBLISHING

First published in 2024 by Bodleian Library Publishing
Broad Street, Oxford OX1 3BG

www.bodleianshop.co.uk

ISBN 978 1 85124 630 4

Publisher: Samuel Fanous
Managing Editor: Susie Foster
Editor: Janet Phillips
Cover design by Dot Little at the Bodleian Library
Designed and typeset by Lucy Morton of illuminati in 10½ on 14 Dante
Printed and bound in China by C&C Offset Printing Co., Ltd.
on 120 gsm Chinese Baijin Pure paper

British Library Catalogue in Publishing Data
A CIP record of this publication is available from the British Library

CONTENTS

My page is white, my ink is black,
My spine is straight; I neatly stack.
Look after me, and treat me kind,
Or under my curse you will find:
My paper cuts, my corners bruise,
Your sight I'll fog, your page I'll lose.
To steer well clear of this affliction,
Heed well the bookish malediction.

INTRODUCTION

None must take this book away,
Nor cut out a page, I'll tell you why,
For it is sacrilege, sirs, I say to you:
He will be cursed in the deed, it's true!

THIS VERSE WAS COMPOSED BY JOHN AUDELAY, A POET
and priest whose collected works are recorded in a manuscript dating to the second quarter of the fifteenth century,
which is now held in the Bodleian Library. Despite the six
hundred years which separate Audelay and the modern
reader, many book lovers will relate to the anxiety of
loaning out a treasured tome. Perhaps, in your darkest
moments, you have even wished harm upon those who
have carried off your books, dog-eared their pages, or
stained their covers with coffee mugs. If so, you are in
good company. Book-owners throughout history have
warned friends and foes alike of the dangers of stealing

or damaging their volumes, and have threatened thieves with everything from hanging and hellfire to sickness and shame. In this book, you will find some of the most gruesome, ingenious and humorous bookish maledictions ever inscribed.

The book curses recorded in this volume draw attention to the most typical as well as the most imaginative of their kind. The curses are ordered chronologically, and range from bookish maledictions inscribed on the monumental stone steles of the ancient Near East to those on bookplates pasted into modern-day paperbacks. You will see that some of the perils promised in book curses have remained popular throughout history: the threat of hanging, for example, appears time and again from the early medieval period onwards. Some book curses, however, are particularly reflective of the time in which they were inscribed and summon the wrath of patron deities, endemic diseases, or well-known execution locations of the period.

In this way, book curses are useful to book historians and literary scholars who seek to understand more about what people thought about writing, and the objects that writing appears on. Book curses can reveal a great deal about the 'book culture' or 'documentary culture' of a particular period or group of people; that is, how they used books and written documents, which texts they thought were valuable and why, and how their books moved between different people and places. They are also eminently entertaining, and their various constructions are testament to the various readers' relationships to their books, and their capacity for imagining violence. Each curse – translated into Modern English, if it was not originally written in it – is accompanied by some detail about the material text that it is found inscribed upon, as well as its cultural and historical significance, to immerse the reader in the bookish landscape from which the curser wrote.

WHAT IS A BOOK CURSE?

A curse is an expression – whether spoken, written or thought – of the desire that someone or something will encounter harm: curses have been documented among the earliest writings of humankind. The term 'book curse' is a slippery one, because not all these types of curse *are* written in books (in this book, you will find curses written on clay tablets and legal documents, as well as codices). What they do all share is a preoccupation with the protection of writing, and of the object upon which the writing sits, often referred to by historians and literary scholars as the 'material text'. The book curses contained in this volume are always conditional: their retributions are only triggered if an individual performs the actions warned against in the curse (for example stealing the book, damaging the book or removing the inscription which details the curse). The curses therefore work as a form of protection that encourages readers to handle inscribed objects with due care and attention, lest they activate the curse's punishment.

Book curses have been recorded and categorized under a variety of different names, and are often labelled as 'colophons', 'ex libris', 'ownership inscriptions', 'dedicatory verses', 'bookplates' or 'book verses' – although these categories encompass more than just book curses alone. Some book curses are referred to as 'anathemas', and indeed many of the curses include the term 'anathema' within the curses themselves. The use of this word often refers to the act of excommunication from the Catholic Church but can also refer to a curse pronounced through or by a deity (usually the Christian God) or, more leniently perhaps, a general declaration that something or something is repulsive and should be condemned by others. This varied categorization and labelling of book curses has meant that they have rarely been considered in conversation with one another. Here, you will find examples of book curses that have been collected together because of their memorable threats, rather than because of the descriptive label they have been given in library or museum catalogues.

Some modern readers might assume that curses are always diabolical in nature – that they call upon dark powers or are written by those allied with evil forces. This, however, is not necessarily the case. For many of the cultures in which these bookish maledictions were written, the power of the curse could be harnessed by the righteous as well as the wicked, and could be used for protection as well as destruction (indeed, many guarantee the former by promising the latter). Many book curses invoke the power of orthodox holy figures, for example the Christian figures of Christ or the Virgin Mary, and were inscribed by pious individuals with religious authority in their communities, such as monks who also served as scribes. Despite this, the punishments threatened in book curses always promise harm to those who breach their terms. These punishments often reflect the concerns of the society in which the curse was written and reveal the kind of threats that would have sent chills down the spines of potential book thieves – precisely because they were eminently plausible, as well as fearsome.

For many of the cultures in which these book curses were written, the ability to read and write was a skill that only a relatively small number of people possessed – those who had the financial means to educate themselves and their children, or who required reading and writing for their professions. For people with limited literacy, the written word was often perceived as a shadowy and half-understood thing wielded by those with particular religious, magical or political power. That does not mean, however, that a belief in the special power of the written word was reserved only for the superstitious, ignorant or unschooled: many cultures throughout history have believed that written charms, spells, prayers and curses could have a significant impact on a reader's life or afterlife, and many have believed the material texts bearing these words to be powerful objects. Consider, for example, the modern-day act of swearing an oath over a book in court, the aim of which is to stop the speaker from committing perjury and incurring the wrath of judicial punishment, in addition to whatever sentence is meted out by their book of choice (whether that be eternal damnation or a guilty conscience).

WHO WROTE BOOK CURSES, WHY WERE THEY WRITTEN, AND WHERE DO I FIND THEM?

In many of the examples collected here, book curses appear within dedicatory inscriptions – inscriptions at the beginning of a handwritten book or document that detail whom it belongs to and sometimes outline the contents of the book – or colophons, which usually appear at the end of an individual text, at the back of a manuscript or on a stone tablet. They may also include the name of the person who gifted the book or asked for it to be created, or the name of the scribe who penned it. The further forward we move through book history the more variable the locations of these book curses become, and they are found scribbled on the margins, included on pages covered in pen trials and doodles, or written in the space where one text ends and another begins, and they appear in printed texts as well as handwritten ones.

The earliest bookish maledictions that we know of are found on clay tablets collected and stored in royal libraries and inscribed upon stone steles: stone monuments erected to commemorate the martial and diplomatic feats of ancient kings. In these cases, anathemas emphasize the power of the rulers who ordered their writing, and preserve their imposing reputations by protecting the material texts on which their exploits were recorded.

Some of the book curses included here are found in manuscripts which would have been expensive to make and to buy. Early medieval manuscripts, for example, were crafted from parchment (the treated skin of animals, usually cows, sheep or goats) with text laboriously penned by hand and illustrated by monks in monastery scriptoria. These books would have taken months, if not years, to complete, and both the materials used to make the book and the labour expended in its construction represent a great deal of investment in terms of money, time and expertise.

Other books warranted the protection of a book curse because they contained secret writings, or those which the owner had spent a great deal of energy and time compiling: for example, those found at the beginning of a fifteenth-century medical handbook, or a seventeenth-century culinary recipe book. Yet more books were guarded because of their sentimental value: perhaps they were gifted by a lover, handed down through generations of a family, or were the favourite possession of a child frequently robbed by their classmates.

Many book curses include the name of the book's owner, the individual who asked for the curse to be inscribed, or the individual who did the inscribing. These different roles were not always embodied by the same person, especially in periods of history where the composer of the text (whom we might now call the 'author') was not the same person who wrote it down. As you will see from the examples given here, book curses were written by men, women and children. The identity of the inscriber, as well as their handwriting style, can offer us insight into which sections of society were literate, who could own books or documents, and how they changed hands between different readers. Because of this, book curses can be a useful way for book historians to understand who owned books during particular periods, and what kinds of text they were reading.

ARE BOOK CURSES FUNNY OR FEARSOME?

The tone of each book curse is dependent on its social and historical context, as well as the kind of material text in which it appears. To a modern reader, the threats contained in some of these curses appear humorously exaggerated, but for the readers of the past these warnings threatened tangible punishments for the theft of property or consequences for their afterlives that, in Christian societies, echoed the sermons they heard in church. The use of rhyme in these curses can also make their violent contents feel playful – modern readers are often more accustomed to rhyme featuring in nursery rhymes, comic poems or songs. For earlier writers, rhyme was used in a range of textual genres, and was a useful means of aiding memorization or emphasizing a particularly important point; it was not necessarily associated with comedy or lightheartedness.

It would be a mistake, however, to think of the writers and readers of the past as devoid of humour. Some of the bookish maledictions included in this book are intentionally humorous, and deliberately feature outdated modes of punishment in more modern textual settings precisely to elicit shock and laughter; for example, those incorporated in the bookplate designs of nineteenth- and twentieth-century book collectors. Others are perhaps less deliberately funny, but comic nonetheless, perhaps especially in the case of those written by children who threaten punishments their small hands would (hopefully) struggle to enact. Book curses therefore often stand in the foggy hinterlands between humour and seriousness. Yet, whether they excite fear, disgust or laughter, they all encourage all of us, the readers, to pause and consider how we value and treat our books.

HOW HAVE THE CURSES IN THIS BOOK BEEN TRANSLATED?

The bookish maledictions dating from antiquity have been given in Modern English only, as these curses have often been through several transliterations (the process of writing words with a different alphabet) and translations to move from the original text to its version in Modern English. These curses are drawn from different scholarly translations, but the names of gods and kings have been standardized for ease of reading. Many of the curses from the early medieval to the early modern periods are written in Latin, and spelling differs between classical Latin and the Latin used in the Middle Ages. For ease of reading, the letter *u* has been changed to *v* if the word has a *v* sound when spoken aloud. Modern punctuation and capitalization (for example, of names and places) has also been added to the Latin, Old English and Middle English curses to help the reader follow the text alongside the Modern English translation. The special characters which feature in the book curses written in Old and Middle English (such as the eth ð, yogh ʒ and thorn þ) have been retained, but any abbreviations have been expanded into the full word. The occasional use of non-standard English or misspelled words which feature in the curses written in Modern English have been retained to preserve the distinctive character of the curse.

For most of the curses, the original setting of the curse on the page (either as verse or as a block of prose) has been retained. However in some cases this has been changed: if the curse rhymes but is presented as a block of prose in its original form, then the curse in its original language as well as the translation into Modern English have been lineated to emphasize the rhyme. Some of the cursers have rendered their book curses with an unusual kind of lineation, particularly child-cursers. In these cases, the original lineation has been kept, but commented on after the translation.

BOOK CURSES
FROM
ANTIQUITY

The 'book curses' written by the scribes of ancient cultures were not written in books, as the technology needed to create the codex had not yet been developed. Instead, they are found written on other text-bearing objects which have survived the test of time, like clay tablets or stone columns or slabs known as steles. Papyrus scrolls were also used throughout Egypt and the Mediterranean during this period, but writings on this material are less likely to survive. The written word was developed by the societies that occupied the ancient Near East – the area which we would now refer to as the Middle East – and the earliest written records have been found inscribed on clay tablets dating shortly before 3000 BCE. The very first writings are practical and factual, documenting numbers of livestock or commodities. They were written in cuneiform, a script that was formed by impressing a wedge-shaped stylus into soft clay (*cunei* in Latin means 'wedge'), which would then dry to create a hard, if somewhat fragile, tablet. These clay tablets could be fired to make them more durable, and some of the tablets which survive today endured because they were inadvertently baked in the plundering fires of war. Writing soon began to be used for more imaginative feats of expression, including technical literature on practising religion and magic, scholarly texts like translation dictionaries, texts about interpreting omens and signs, and literary texts like the *Epic of Gilgamesh*.

The curses found inscribed on objects of the ancient Near East show us that these societies had interesting ideas about the power of writing, and also about the power of the objects which bore writing. They reveal that people often viewed material texts as physical representations of their contents: the creation and destruction of an inscribed stone stele, for example, reflected the making and breaking of laws or treaties by people. They also show an acute awareness of the importance of the word for preserving the memory of individuals and their great acts (whether that is founding a city or destroying one), and they often promise harsh punishments to those who erase names, or who supplant them with their own. The curses are lengthy when compared to their later bookish counter-parts, and their listing of the many ways a text can be destroyed can read as a little excessive to modern eyes. It is worth remembering, however, that these inscriptions were ordered by kings intent on conveying their military might and their divinely sanctioned power – and the more expansive the list of punishments, the more impressively formidable the king.

THE CURSE OF YAHDUN-LIM'S
TEMPLE DEDICATION

Whoever desecrates this temple, assigns it to evil and untoward purposes, does not reinforce its foundation, does not replace what has fallen down or stops the food offerings [destined] for it, erases my name [in this inscription] – or gives orders for erasing it – and inscribes his own name not previously inscribed – or gives orders for writing it – or prompts somebody else [to do these things] on account of the curses [inscribed here], be this man a king, or a general, or a mayor, or whoever else, Enlil who pronounces decisions for [all] the gods should make the kingdom of this man smaller than that of all the other kings; Sin, the elder brother among the gods, his brothers, should curse him with the 'Great Curse'; Nergal, the armed god, should break his weapon and not accept him [in the nether world when he appears there] slain [in battle]; Ea, the master of fates, should make his fate a bad one; the great lady, Aja the Bride, should forever represent his case in a bad light before Shamash; Bunene, the great plenipotentiary of Shamash, should end his life, eliminate every offspring of his, so that neither descendant nor progeny of his should ever live under the sun.

Yahdun-Lim was the king of Mari, a city-state in modern-day Syria, between 1820 and 1796 BCE. After a successful military campaign against various nomad groups, Yahdun-Lim dedicated a temple to Shamash, the god of the sun and of justice. In 1953 the archaeologist André Parrot excavated the Royal Palace at Mari and unearthed nine terracotta bricks which detailed the long dedication of the temple, and included this curse.

THE CURSE OF
HAMMURABI'S LAW STELE

If the aforementioned man [the future king] does
not listen to my words, which I inscribed upon my
narû; if he forgets my ways and does not respect the
ways of the gods; and if he overturns the judgment,
which I judged; if he changes my words, which I
inscribed; if he removes my designs; if he erases
my inscribed name and inscribes his own name ...
May the great god Anu, father of the gods, who has
proclaimed my reign, deprive him of the sheen of
royalty, smash his sceptre, and curse his destiny!

This curse features on the law stele of the Babylonian king
Hammurabi, who reigned from around 1792 to 1750 BCE; it
was discovered at the site of the ancient city of Susa in the
modern-day Khuzestan province of Iran. Hammurabi's stele,
which is referred to as a *narû* in the curse, is carved from black
basalt and stands at just over 2 metres high. At the top of the
stele is a relief of Hammurabi and Shamash, the Babylonian
god of justice and the sun. The cuneiform text inscribed below
the relief explains that Hammurabi was appointed king by the
gods, and then outlines the punishment one could expect for
breaking various laws.

THE CURSE OF A
SEFIRE TREATY STELE

Whoever will not observe the words of the inscription
which is on this stele or will say 'I shall efface some
of its words', or 'I shall upset the good relations and
turn them to evil', on any day on which he will do
so, may the gods overturn that man and his house
and all that is in it. May they make its lower part
its upper part! May his scion inherit no name!

This curse is written on the first of three steles discovered in
As-Safira (referred to by locals as Sfire), a city near Aleppo in
Syria. The three basalt steles date to the eighth century BCE,
and bear Aramaic inscriptions that detail a treatise made between two Assyrian kings, Bar-Ga'yah and Mati'el. The curse
of the stele offers two frightening consequences: the dizzying
threat that the perpetrator's world shall be turned topsy-turvy
by the gods (presumably in the metaphorical sense, but a literal
interpretation is just as terrifying), and the threat that any
claim to a grand legacy will perish with them.

THE CURSE OF SHALMANESER IV'S COMMEMORATION STELE

As for my stele, you must not remove it from its place, or put it somewhere else. You must not put it in a Taboo House, you must not smash it, you must not cover it with earth, you must not throw it into water, you must not splash bitumen on it, you must not burn it, you must not erase my inscription ... As for the one who alters my inscription or my name, may the gods Ashur, Shamas, Marduk and Adad, the great gods, not have mercy upon him, to his utter destruction.

Shalmaneser IV was the king of the Neo-Assyrian Empire from 783 to 773 BCE. Unearthed at Tell Abta, an archaeological site near Lake Tharthar in modern-day Iraq, the stone stele bearing this curse commemorates the founding of a new city in the desert. The curse refers to bitumen, a naturally occurring form of petroleum that appeared in deposits across Mesopotamia. There is evidence of its use as an adhesive for construction and as waterproofing for boats and baskets, but it is also a very flammable material – perhaps this explains the curse's warning against splashing bitumen on the stele directly before that of burning. Four gods are invoked by name in this curse: the national god of the ancient Assyrians, Ashur; the omnipotent sun god, Shamas; the god of Babylon, Marduk; and the storm and rain god, Adad.

THE CURSE OF SARGON II'S
MEMORIAL STELE

In days to come, may some future prince look upon
my memorial stele, may he read it, the name of the
great gods may he honour, let him anoint my stele
with oil, pour out libations, let him not change its
location. Whoever destroys my stele, blots out my
name or inscription, may all the great gods, whose
names are named upon this stele, and the gods who
dwell in the midst of the great sea, curse him with an
evil curse, his name and his seed may they destroy
in the land. May they have no mercy upon him.

Sargon II ruled the Neo-Assyrian Empire between 722 and 705
BCE and ordered this stele to be erected around 707 BCE. The
stele, which is made of basalt, reinforces the power of Sargon
by recounting his many military and diplomatic successes.
The stele was unearthed in 1845 in the modern-day city of
Larnaca in Cyprus, and was offered to the British Museum for
£20, but was instead sold to the Berlin State Museum for the
equivalent of £50.

A CURSE FROM THE LIBRARY
OF ASHURBANIPAL

Palace of Ashurbanipal, King of the World,
King of Assyria, who trusts in Ashur and Ninlil.
Whoever trusts in you will not be shamed, king
of the gods, Ashur! Whoever takes [this tablet]
away, or writes his own name instead of mine,
may Ashur and Ninlil wildly and furiously reject
him, and destroy his name and seed in the land!

Ashurbanipal, king of the Neo-Assyrian Empire from around
661 to 639 BCE, was a fearsome military ruler, the founder of
an expansive and pioneering library, and the last of the great
Assyrian kings. Over 30,000 clay tablets in various states of
fragmentation were found in the ancient city of Ninevah
(within the modern city of Mosul in northern Iraq) bearing
cuneiform writings. The discovery of the library is credited
to Austen Henry Layard but was aided by Hormuzd Rassam,
a Mosul native who continued to excavate in Ninevah after
Layard left to pursue a political career.

The library of Ashurbanipal was a personal royal collection,
although it is likely that scribes, priests and other professionals
had access to it; hence the existence of the protective curses
inscribed on some of the tablets. Among the writings are
administrative documents, texts on omens and divinations,
medicinal and astrological works, and literary epics and myths.
Notably, the collection contains the *Epic of Gilgamesh,* the epic

poem that recounts the heroic deeds of Gilgamesh, who was sent by the gods to free the Uruk people.

Most of the tablets are now in London's British Museum, and scholars continue their efforts to catalogue and understand the complex collection which was irreparably muddled on its journey across Europe.

Early Medieval
Book Curses

The curses featured in this chapter belong to the Early Middle Ages of Europe: the period after the decline of the Western Roman Empire and leading up to the High Middle Ages (roughly 500 CE to 1100 CE). The earlier part of this period has sometimes been referred to as the 'Dark Ages', a pejorative term used to characterize these years as a time of senseless brutality, cultural decline and a lack of written records. This portrayal has largely been debunked. During this period continental Europe bore witness to the glittering Byzantine Empire in the east and the south, the Golden Age of Islam and its advanced learning, and the rule of the Carolingian dynasty. Early medieval England saw the arrival of the Saxons from north-west Europe, Viking invasions, and the slow unification of a kingdom. Great works of literature were written in Old English – like the epic poem *Beowulf*, the riddles of the Exeter Book and *The Anglo-Saxon Chronicle* – and in Latin, which was largely used for administrative writing and theological texts.

Book curses from this period appear in codices and in legal documents, such as wills, land grants and administrative letters. In early medieval England legal agreements were performed in oral ceremonies and afterwards documented in writing. Most of these legal documents do not survive in their original form but were transcribed into cartularies (collections of legal documents compiled for posterity). Most of the curses that feature in these legal documents threaten those who act to violate their terms – for example, the seizing of land promised to another – rather than those who act to destroy the document or edit its text, but the two examples which feature in this book are clearly concerned with the destruction of the physical document.

The curses found written in books, by contrast, are largely concerned with theft, but also with the concealment of the theft (perhaps by being an accessory to the crime, or deliberately obfuscating the stolen book's location), and the removal of the ownership inscription that shows who the book rightly belongs to. The written documents that survive from this period were most commonly produced by monks working in scriptoria – rooms in monasteries reserved for the penning of texts and the illustrating of books. Correspondingly, the book curses from this period are invariably inscribed by monks who dedicate their books to the community that they belong to, and their cloistered environments do not seem to have confined their capacity for viciousness.

One distinctive phrase found in many of the Latin book curses of this period, and of later ages too, is *anathema marathana*. The Aramaic phrase *marathana* is generally translated as an invocation to God, 'Oh Lord, come!', or a thunderous statement, 'the Lord has come' (the equivocation comes from the fact that the word is a transliteration – a swapping of letters from the Aramaic alphabet to the Greek alphabet). Together, the words *anathema marathana* are somewhere between an earnest prayer that the transgressor is cursed by God and an assured pronouncement that they are. Indeed, the two words are menacingly chant-like: the twin four-syllable words with only one letter different are reminiscent of the more commonly recognized *abracadabra* and *hocus-pocus*, words which also have obscure etymologies.

THE CURSE OF
BISHOP ÆLFSIGA'S WILL

If anyone does so [alters this will], may God
destroy him both soul and body, both here and
in the future, unless I myself change it.

*Gif hit þonne hwa do God hine fordo ge mid
sawle ge mid lichoman ge her ge on ban to
feondan buton io hit self on ober wcende.*

Ælfsiga was the Bishop of Winchester from 951 to 958, before
he became the Archbishop of Canterbury. Ælfsiga froze to
death while trying to cross the Alps to collect his pallium, an
ecclesiastical vestment, from the Pope in Rome as part of a
profession of faith. His will was written just a year before his
death in 959.

THE CURSE OF KING ÆTHELRED'S LAND GRANT

If, truly, anyone swollen with the lust of cupidity
shall attempt to destroy this my charter of
donation, let him be anathema maranatha –
that is, excluded from the fellowship of Christians
– unless he comes to his senses and, repenting,
does penance for what he tried to do fraudulently.

Si quis Vero cupiditatis zelo inflatus hunc
mee donationis libellum destruere temptaverit,
sit anathema maranatha, hoc est alienatio a
consortio Christianorum, nisi resipuerit et quod
callide facere temptaverit penitens penituerit.

This curse features in a grant that transfers land from King Æthelred II (also known as King Æthelred the Unready) to a lord called Æthelwig. The grant explains that Æthelwig has been given the land after intervening in the proceedings of a complicated robbery gone wrong, whereby a bridle was stolen and two brothers were beaten to death (whom Æthelwig proceeded to bury as Christians). For his service, Æthelwig was granted land in Ardley, Oxfordshire. The grant does not survive in its original form but in a manuscript known as *The Cartulary and Customs of Abingdon Abbey*, which also contains beautifully colourful and detailed illustrations of historical and Christian figures. The grant, which is largely written in Latin, switches to Old English to describe the bounds of the land being given.

CONSTANTIUS' BOOK CURSE

I, Constantius, the sinner and unworthy priest
of St Peter's of Luxeuil, wrote these books
of Boethius on geometry to serve him ... at
the command of the pious Father Milo. So
let there be grace for the user, forgiveness for
the scribe and anathema to the swindler.

*Ego Constantius peccator et indignus sacerdos
sancti Petri Luxoviensis coenobii scripsi ad
serviendum ei hos libros Boetii de Geometria
... praecepto pii patris Milonis. Sit ergo utenti
gratia, scriptori venia, fraudatori anathema.*

This bookish malediction is inscribed in an early-eleventh-
century manuscript containing a geometry text, wrongly
attributed to Boethius. The scribe Constantius was part of
the Benedictine community of Luxeuil, an abbey that was
established by the Irish missionary St Columbán, built on the
site of an old Roman fort called Luxovium.

THE LATIN AND
OLD ENGLISH BOOK CURSE OF
BISHOP LEOFRIC OF EXETER

This book was given by Leofric, Bishop of St Peter
the Apostle in Exeter, his episcopal see, for the relief
of his soul, and for the benefit of his successors.
But if anyone removes it from there, let them
lie under perpetual malediction. So be it!

Hunc librum dat Leofricus episcopus ecclesiae
Sancti Petri Apostoli in Exonia ad sedem suam
episcopalem, pro remedio anime sue, ad utilitatem
successorum suorum. Siquis autem ilium inde
abstulerit, perpetue maledictioni subiaceat. fiat.

This book was given by Leofric, Bishop of St Peter's
minster in Exeter, where his episcopal see is, for the
use of his successors. And if anyone removes it, may
he have eternal publishment with all the devils. Amen.

Ðas boc gef leofric biscop into Sancte Petres mynstre þær
his biscopstol is his æfterfiligendum to nitweorðnysse.
gif hie hwa utætbrede, hæbbe he ece geniðerunge
mid eallum deoflum. Amen.

This book curse appears in an eleventh-century manuscript
gifted to Exeter Cathedral by Bishop Leofric. Leofric became
Bishop of Exeter in 1050, and King Edward the Confessor

attended his enthronement. Leofric was responsible for expanding the collection and production of books at Exeter Cathedral, and nine surviving early medieval manuscripts contain a famous 'Leofric Inscription' marking them as a gift from the bishop to the Cathedral. This example of Leofric's curse is written in both Latin and Old English, perhaps as insurance against any thief who claims they should be excused damnation because they only understand one of the languages.

A BOOK CURSE THREATENING
HELL'S POSSESSION

The work which was begun
[by Father Odbert] I finished.
I pray that, from this book, there may
be great peace for Father Odbert,
And that there may be salvation
for all those living in Saint-Omer.
Whoever aided me, may he flourish in Christ.
May hell possess anyone who steals me from here.

Istud opus coeptum domino patrante peregi.
Pax sit multi patri precor Odberto super album,
Sitque salus cunctis Sithiu de gentibus omnis.
In Christo ualeat. Mihi quisque iuvamen adauxit.
Tartara possideant me quisque furavreit ex hinc.

This bookish malediction is found in a manuscript produced
by monks at the Abbey of Saint Bertin in Saint-Omer, France,
which is now in ruins. Father Odbert was abbot of the abbey
between around 986 and 1007 CE and supported the development of the scriptorium there, copying the texts contained in
many of the manuscripts himself. The first letter of every line
of the full Latin inscription that contains this curse forms an
acrostic that translates as 'Heriveus wrote me for St Bertin'.

A BOOK CURSE BLESSING SCRIBES
AND PUSHING THIEVES INTO HELL

It is not one hand that offers you this gift, O Pastor.
Accept the written book, St Vedast.
Look after the scribes,
making them blessed after death.
He who shall have snatched [the book] by stealth,
push powerfully to hell.

Hoc non una manus offert pastor tibi munus.
Accipe perscriptum Sancta Vedaste librum.
Serva punctigraphos faciens post fata beatos.
Qui tulerit furto. trude potens baratro.

This book curse is found in an eleventh-century manuscript
owned by the Benedictine Abbey of Saint Vedast in Arras,
France. Saint Vedast was a bishop in the sixth century and is
the patron saint of eye difficulties (perhaps useful to scribes
working long hours in dimly lit scriptoria). This manuscript
contains a work by the Roman senator Cassiodorus, who
established a great monastery at Vivarium that centred around
book production.

A BOOK CURSE
COMPARING CHRIST'S BODY
TO A MANUSCRIPT PAGE

As I write the book, Vedast looks down from the
uppermost regions of heaven and notes how many
letters I trace with my pens, with how many lines
the page is furrowed and how many sharp points
the folio is wounded on this side and on that. And
then looking favourably on our work and on our
labour, he says: 'As many letters as there are, as many
lines as there are, and finally as many prickings as
there are in this book, so many sins I now remit for
you – Christ grants that I have this eternal power'
… For this reward I industriously wrote this book,
which if anyone should carry off, may the earth below
gape open for him so that, living, he may proceed to
darksome hell with raging fires. So be it. So be it.

Cum librum scribo. Vedastus ab aethere summo respicit e
caelis, notat et quot grammata notris depingam calamis. quot
aretur pagina sulcis, quot folium punctis. hinc hinc laceratur
acutis. tuncque favens operi nostro nostroque labori.
grammata quot, sulci quot sunt quot denique puncti inquit.
in hoc libro; tot crimina iam tibi dono; hanque potestatem
dat Christus habere perhennem … Hac mercede librum per
scripsi sedulus istum. quem si quis tollat; tellus huic dehiscat
vivus ut infernum petat amplis ignibus atrum. Fiat Fiat.

This book curse appears as part of a dedicatory verse written at the beginning of a manuscript dating from the second quarter of the eleventh century, and that contains a commentary on the Psalms. The manuscript was made by a monk and copyist named Rudolphus, who belonged to the Benedictine order of the Abbey of Saint Vedast in Arras, France. Rudolphus is drawn at the top of the page sitting at a writing desk and holding a quill pen, his inkhorn open. Opposite him is the rather fearsomely depicted St Vedast, who writes on his own scroll and looks down at Rudolphus from heaven. The beginning of the curse draws an oblique parallel between Christ's body and the constituent parts of a book, down to the 'prickings' used to mark the side of a page and make evenly spaced straight lines.

High Medieval
Book curses

The book curses of this chapter date between 1100 and 1350 CE, a period which can be loosely defined as the High Middle Ages of Europe. In the year 1212 the Council of Paris, a council called and attended by Catholic authorities, banned the use of anathemas intended to stop the theft of books. This ruling appears to have been largely ignored. Amusingly, all the curses included in this section are featured in manuscripts that belonged to monasteries or nunneries of different Christian religious orders. The curses most commonly feature the threat of excommunication, a pronouncement that would have been significant to both contemplative communities and members of the laity harbouring thievish intentions, but they sometimes generously include a clause that the thief will be excused if they return the book and repent. Others are not so kind, and promise death to the book thief. The maledictions of this period often express a concern with community: they usually name the institution to which the book belongs, and some of the curses read as if the manuscript is itself insisting that it should not be removed from the company of its bookish brethren. It was in these years that the first universities, including Oxford, began to emerge (the oldest of them all being the University of Bologna), and at least one of the manuscripts featured in this chapter was used by a student at university.

Outside of the confines of the cloister, medieval Europe bore witness to historical events and literary developments that feature most vividly in our modern-day imagining of the period. The most famous of the Catholic Crusades were waged in the Holy Land between the eleventh and thirteenth centuries, and Christians and Muslims both used the fighting to bolster religious and national mythologies. This period also saw the development of the chivalric code, which combined elements of Christianity with those of knighthood, and influenced the behaviour of men of high social standing. Some of the best-known romance literature of this period, such as the Arthurian works of Chrétien de Troyes and the allegorical poem *Le Roman de la Rose,* offer a commentary on the chivalric values of loyalty, honour and valour.

A BOOK CURSE REPEATED
EVERY YEAR BY CANDLELIGHT

The book of the Church of St Mary's
in Abingdon. Whoever steals me: let him be
anathema. This sentence is repeated every year
in the chapter, with a book and a candle.

*Liber ecclesie Sancte Marie de Abbendone. Quicumque
ipsum alienaverit anathema sit. Hic sentencia singulis
annis data est in capitulo cum libro et candela.*

This book curse is written in a manuscript that belonged to the
Benedictine Abbey of St Mary the Virgin in Abingdon, a town
which sits a few miles outside Oxford. The manuscript dates
to the first quarter of the twelfth century (although the book
curse itself dates to the late thirteenth century), and contains
a range of theological texts, many of them centred around the
Eucharist. The curse states that it is repeated once a year, and
with two very particular objects: a book and a candle. This
could be a reference to the ceremony of excommunication,
which was sometimes performed with a bell, a book and
a candle, which were respectively, rung, clapped shut and
extinguished at the conclusion of the ceremony. It could also
be a reference to the common monastic practice of reading
through the entire liturgy once a year, at which point the curse
would be spoken once again.

ABBOT SIMON'S BOOK CURSE

Simon, Abbot of Saint Albans, had this book
written, and whoever steals it or destroys
its inscription: let him be anathema.

Hunc librum fecit dominus Symon Abbas
Sancto Albano, quem qui ei abstulerit aut
titulum hunc deleverit: anathema sit.

The manuscript containing this book curse dates from the
second half of the twelfth century, and contains a commentary on the book of Leviticus from the Bible (that is, a text
designed to help the reader interpret a particular passage) by
the Benedictine monk Ralph of Flavigny. The book was made
for Simon, Abbot of St Albans between 1167 and 1183, and book
curses that include his name are found in several manuscripts
of the period. The manuscript was given to Trinity Hall,
Cambridge, by Robert Hare, a famous antiquary of the late
sixteenth century.

THE BOOK CURSE OF THE ABBEY OF
SAINTS MARY & NICHOLAS, ARNSTEIN

The book of the Abbey of Saints Mary and Nicholas
of Arnstein. Whoever steals it: may he die a
death, may he be cooked in a frying pan, may the
falling sickness and fever attack him, and may
he be rotated [on a wheel] and hanged. Amen.

Liber Sancte Marie Sancti que Nycolai in Arrinstein.
Quem si quis abstulerit morte moriatur, in
sartagine coquatur, caducus morbus instet eum
et febres, et rotatur et suspendatur. Amen.

The manuscript containing this book curse is known as 'The
Arnstein Bible' after the Abbey of Saint Mary & Saint Nicholas
in Arnstein, north-west Germany. The manuscript contains
the first books of the Bible from Genesis to Malachi, and was
penned in 1172 or 1173 by a monk named Lunandus. The book
curse appears at the end of the manuscript on a folio which has
largely been cut away from the book, but whoever took a blade
to the page was careful enough to leave the curse behind. The
curse threatens several punishments towards thieves, notably
that of *caducus morbus,* the 'falling sickness', the name commonly given to what we would now call epilepsy. The curse
also states that the thief should be *rotatur,* 'rotated', referring
to the punishment enacted on a breaking wheel (also known
as a Catherine Wheel after St Catherine of Alexandria, who
was threatened with the wheel but managed to break it with a
single touch). Victims would be tied to the wheel and clubbed,
often until death, and then displayed.

THE BOOK CURSE OF
SANTA MARIA DELLA COLOMBA

The book of St Mary of the Dove.
Whoever steals or removes [this book]:
let him be anathema. Amen.

Liber Sancte Marie de Columba.
Quicumque eum furatus fuerit.
Vel alienaverit. Anathema sit. Amen

This book curse is found on a fragment of a twelfth-century manuscript that contained Pope Gregory I's *Homiliæ in evangelia*, a collection of homilies on the gospels. The book once belonged to the monastery of Santa Maria della Colomba, or Saint Mary of the Dove, a Cistercian monastery in northern Italy. Its unusual name alludes to the foundation myth of the monastery, whereby a white dove supposedly signalled the place where it should be built. The dove also features in many high medieval visual representations of Mary, where it appears within a ray of light at the Annunciation.

THE BOOK CURSE OF THE
ABBEY OF MONT-SAINT-QUENTIN

In the name of the Father, the Son and the Holy
Ghost, Amen. In the one thousand, two hundred
and twenty-nine years since the incarnation of
our Lord, Peter (the least of all the monks) offered
this book to the martyr Quintus. If anyone
removes it: on the Day of Judgement, before the
presence of our Lord Jesus Christ, let him feel
that the most holy martyr accuses against him.

*In nomine patris et filii et spiritus sancti, amen.
anno ab incarnatione domini millesimo ducentesimo
uicesimo nono Petrus monachorum omnium minimus
obtulit istum librum beatissimo martiri Quintino. si
quis eum abstulerit in die iudicii ante conspectum
domini nostri Ihesu Christi ipsum sanctissimum
martirem contra se accusatorem sentiat.*

This book curse is both visually colourful and prominently
placed in the thirteenth-century manuscript in which it is
inscribed. The malediction forms the text of the presentation
page (the page which details who presented the book): it is
written in rows alternating between bright blue and orange,
and is topped with a detailed architectural scene.

The manuscript contains a work by the twelfth-century
French theologian Petrus Comestor called the *Historia
scholastica*, a text which offers an overview of biblical history

and which was later used as a university textbook. Comestor's name is sometimes translated into English as 'Peter the Eater' (*comestor* in Latin means 'the eater'). Comestor supposedly composed his own epitaph, in which he makes a pun of his name. Translated into English, the first lines read:

> I was Peter, whom this stone covers,
> called 'devourer', now I am devoured.

THE YEAR-LONG BOOK CURSE
OF ROCHESTER PRIORY

Whoever steals this book from the cloister, conceals
its theft or fraudulently erases its inscription incurs
the damnation of anathema from the priory and
the entire chapter of Rochester for one long year.

Hunc librum quicumque alienaverit ab hoc claustro,
alienatum celaverit, uel hunc titulum in fraudem
deleverit, dampnacionem incurrit anathematis lati
singulis armis a priore et totu cetu capituli Roffens.

This book curse appears in a late-thirteenth-century manuscript containing some of Aristotle's works on physics. These
texts have been glossed (annotated with brief explanation) by
a student at Oxford University, who leaves a Latin inscription
noting that 'Henry de Renham wrote this book and heard it
lectured on in the schools at Oxford, and emended and glossed
it whilst listening to the lectures.' This book, as the curse
states, belonged to Rochester Priory, the inhabitants of which
were prodigious book-cursers – many manuscripts that were
in their ownership still bear their haunting threats.

THE BOOK CURSE OF
ROBERT OF ALDSWORTH

Robert of Aldsworth had this book written.
I am for the community;
I do not want to be separated.
May I therefore be given to one,
as I am available to all.
Whoever steals me or removes me: he will be cursed.
The penalty for that person is anathema.

Hunc librum fecit scribi Robertus de Aldeswyrth.
Sum de communi. nolo fieri specialis.
Tradar sic uni quod cunctis sim generalis.
Qui me furatus fuerit aut alienaverit. sit ille maledictus.
Plectatur pena tali quod sit anathema.

This book curse is written in a thirteenth-century Bible that
once belonged to Robert of Aldsworth, a monk from Gloucester Cathedral, which was then known as the Abbey of St Peter.
The curse is written in a very clear script on the front inside
binding, opposite a folio listing other books owned by Robert.
Aside from the first line proclaiming Robert's ownership
the curse is written in the first person, as if the book itself is
speaking and declaring its wish to remain with the fellowship
of books written on the following page.

THE BOOK CURSE OF THE *ANCRENE WISSE*

The book of the Church of Saint James of Wigmore.
John Purcel gave this book to the church at the
insistence of Brother Walter of Lodelawe, the
senior precentor. Whoever steals this book or
erases this inscription: let them be anathema.
Amen. So be it, so be it, so be it. Amen.

Liber ecclesie S. Jacobi de Wygemore. quem Johannes
Purcel dedit eidem ecclesie ad instanciam fratris Walteri
de Lodelawe senioris tunc precentoris. Siquis dictum
librum alienaverit a predicta ecclesia. uel titulum hunc
maliciose deleverit anathema. Amen. Fiat fiat fiat. Amen.

This book curse appears at the bottom of the first folio of a
manuscript containing the *Ancrene Wisse*, a guide for anchoresses. Anchoresses were women who chose to withdraw from
society to live a life of deep piety in an anchoritic cell adjoined
to a church. This small room would have three windows: one
called a 'squint' or 'hagioscope' through which she could view
church services, one which enabled her to receive the necessi-
ties of living, and another which faced the outside world. The
cell was likened to both womb and tomb, as the anchoress's
new identity began in that space, which would later become
the place that she died. Other books belonging to the Church
of St James also contain amusing book curses: another states
that the book thief shall be anathema until they come to their
senses and make amends with the robbed.

THE CURSE OF THE ABBEY OF
ST MARY THE VIRGIN,
ROBERTSBRIDGE

The book of St Mary's, Robertsbridge. Whoever steals it, sells it, or in any other way removes it or cuts away any part of it: let him be anathema. Maranatha. Amen.

Liber sancte Marie de Ponte Roberti. Qui eum
abstulerit, aut vendiderit, uel quolibet modo ab
hac domo alienaverit uel quamlibet eius partem
absciderit, sit Anathema. Maranatha. Amen

This book curse is written on the final folio of a thirteenth-century manuscript containing many works attributed to Augustine of Hippo. The curse has been crossed out (both through every line, and then in a large cross over the entire curse), but the underlying text is still legible. Below the curse is a later inscription by John Grandisson, Bishop of Exeter, who states that he does not know where the above-named church is, and that he did not steal the book but acquired it by legitimate means. Other later inscriptions in the book also provide an insight into the book culture of universities in fourteenth-century England. The first folio of the manuscript bears several partially expunged pledge or *caucio* notes, meaning that the manuscript was held as collateral for a loan. These books would be stored in chests until the loan was cleared, or would be forfeited to the chest-keeper; one of the pledge notes here states that the book was placed into the *Cista Universitatis* (the 'university chest'), likely that of Oxford University.

A SIMPLE BOOK CURSE
THREATENING HANGING

Whoever steals this book
will be hanged by the neck.

Qui librum furatur
per collum pendere datur

This concise book curse, which rhymes in its original Latin, is inscribed in a thirteenth-century manuscript containing a psalter and a hymnary (which were formally two separate manuscripts). The manuscript belonged to the community of nuns at Campsey Priory in Suffolk. Some of the prayers have been specifically adapted for a female readership or audience.

A BOOK CURSE PRAISING SCRIBES
AND DAMNING THIEVES

Here ends the Book of the Passion.
Thanks be to God.
Those who write, let them write;
may they always live with God.
Whoever steals me,
return me, or die.

Explicit liber
passionarii deo gratias.
Qui scripsit scribat
semper cum domino vivat.
Qui me furatur
vel reddat vel moriatur

The first lines of this colophon are a common rhyming scribal prayer but, unusually, this scribe has decided to add on a further rhyming threat to book thieves. The curse appears in a manuscript dating from the second half of the thirteenth century, with some later additions from the early fourteenth century, and was part of a Roman lectionary belonging to the papal library of the Palais des Papes in Avignon, France. The Palais was the papal residence from 1306 to 1377, and was an important site in the turbulent Papal Schism of the late fourteenth century, when two (and briefly three) popes vied for supremacy.

THE BOOK CURSE
OF NEWARK PRIORY

This book belongs to the Church of St Mary and
the blessed St Thomas the Martyr in New Place.
Whoever has taken [this book] away or has in any
way removed it without the knowledge of that
church: let him be anathema maranatha. Amen.

*Hic liber est ecclesie sancte Marie et beati Thome
martiris de nouo loco. quem qui furto abstulerit vel
sine consciencia eiusdem ecclesie conventus quocumque
modo alienaverit sit anathema maranatha. amen*

This book curse is that of Newark Priory, which now sits in
ruins on an island in the middle of the River Wey in Surrey.
The curse uses the name *novo loco* to describe its location,
which literally translates into English as 'new place', now
Newark. The manuscript that this curse is found in contains
two works of the twelfth-century historian William of Malm-
esbury: the *Gesta regum Anglorum* (the Deeds of the Kings of the
English) and the *Historia nouella*. The curse is mostly erased,
but is visible under UV light and matches that of another
manuscript from Newark Priory.

LATE MEDIEVAL BOOK CURSES

IN THE LATER MEDIEVAL PERIOD, BOOK PRODUCTION began to move out of monastery scriptoria and into towns and cities; professional scribes were often employed to pen texts commissioned by keen readers. The ability to read and write increased among the middle classes and resulted in the penning of books which contained texts relating to an individual's particular interests – such as medicine, household or gardening knowledge, crafts, poetry or the esoteric arts. There is also a greater use of Middle English, as opposed to Latin, as the vernacular (the language commonly spoken) increasingly began to be used in writing too. The books included in this chapter reflect the wide range of texts that were being copied or created during this period and their equally varied readership: there are curses in a medical practitioner's handbook and a noble woman's book of hours (a book of prayers to be recited at set times of the day); a book of sermons and a collection of texts on alchemy and palmistry.

This period represents the golden age of book cursing, and the bookish maledictions that you will find here are as varied as they are violent. Hanging is the most common punishment threatened in later medieval curses, and this perhaps reflects the visibility of hanged criminals. In later medieval Europe, hanging was achieved with a 'short drop' (as opposed to the 'long drop' implemented in later years with a trap door) by kicking a ladder or cart out from under a victim's legs or hoisting them up by the neck. These executions would mostly be performed outside the city walls but in a prominent location like a hill, and the dead bodies of the criminals were sometimes displayed in gibbets (dangling human-shaped cages) to deter others from committing similar crimes. There are various terms describing the accoutrements of hanging in these curses, such as 'gallows', 'tree' and 'hook'.

A BOOK CURSE IN A MANUSCRIPT CONTAINING VOLVELLES

The book of St Mary's of Boxley, acquired
by the owner John Heriettsham from the
executors of John Renham, the late rector of
Holingbourne. Whoever maliciously steals it:
let him be anathema maranatha. Amen.

*liber S. Marie de Boxele, emptus per dompnum
Jo. heriettsham ab executoribus m. Jo. Renham nuper
rectoris de holyngbourne. in quem qui maliciose
alienaverit anathema sit maranatha. Amen.*

This book curse is written on the first folio of an early-fourteenth-century manuscript that contains a variety of secular texts, including astronomical tables, zodiac predictions, a list of the values of wool in various counties and materials related to London *eyres*, the circuits which judicial courts or itinerant justices visited. The manuscript contains several intricately drawn diagrams, and includes two astrological volvelles (wheel charts) which have been sewn in. The curse has been erased and is now very faint.

JOHN WRYGHTSON'S BOOK CURSE

This book is one,
Christ's curse is another;
He who steals the one,
I pray well that he is sent the other.
Said John Wryghtson.

Thys boke ys on,
crystys curs ys Anodyr;
he that stellyth the ton,
I pray good send hym þe todyr.
quod Iohannes Wryghtson.

This book curse is written in a medical practitioner's hand-book dating from the middle of the fourteenth century. It largely consists of the *Chirurgia*, a thirteenth-century text on surgery by the Italian surgeon William of Saliceto, who was well-known for favouring the use of a scalpel over cauteriza-tion (the burning of the flesh to stop infection). It also contains important prayers, biblical quotations and hymns, along with drawings of surgical instruments.

THE GONVILLE & CAIUS COLLEGE BOOK CURSE

Wherever I end up, overall,
I belong to the Chapel of Gonville Hall;
He that wickedly went and took me away
Shall be cursed by the Great Sentence.
And whether he carried me in a sleeve or a sack,
For my sake he shall be hanged by the neck,
(For I am so easily recognized by different men)
Unless I am restored there again.

Where so ever y be come over all
I belonge to the Chapell of Gunvylle hall;
He shall be cursed by the grate-sentens
That felonsly faryth and berith me thens.
And whether he bere me in pooke or sekke,
For me he shall be hanged by the nekke,
(I am so well beknown of dyverse men)
But I be restored theder again.

The curse is written in a fourteenth-century breviary, a lit-urgical book containing prayers and readings that would have been recited at regular points of the day and night as part of the canonical hours. The poetic voice of the curse is that of the book itself, which lends the foreboding impression that the manuscript itself is a conscious being. The 'Great Sentence' promised in the third line of the curse likely refers to the punishment of excommunication, which was often called the Great Curse. The Middle English term *pooke* can refer to either a bag or a sleeve; if the remark alludes to the smuggling of books in sleeves, it is perhaps a reference to the elongated and voluminous sleeves of the *houppelande*, a garment fashionable among the gentry and nobility in the fourteenth century, or the capacious sleeves of monk's habits, which could easily conceal a book.

A BOOK CURSE THREATENING ILLNESS IN THIS LIFE AND ETERNAL DAMNATION IN THE NEXT

This is the book of the Abbey of Blessed Mary of Titchfield, of the Premonstratensian Order, in the diocese of Winton near Portsmouth, in the county of Southampton. Whoever from that place steals me by fraud, or donation, or by sale, or who by any other means or colour removes me or keeps me from the abbey of the same name, or who has erased this inscription, or who provided advice, help, or agreed to any of the previous actions: let his name be removed from the Book of Life, and in this and the age to come, may he know infirmity and eternal damnation. Furthermore, he and all his accomplices are anathema maranatha. So be it, so be it – it is written. Amen.

Hic est liber abbathie beate Marie de Tychefelde, ordinis Premonstratensis, Wyntoniensis diocesis iuxta Portesmuthe in comitatu Suthampton. quem qui ab eadem per fraudem, vel per donacionem, aut per vendicionem seu alio quoquo modo vel colore alienaverit siue retinuerit qnominus eiusdem abbatie sit, seu qui hunc titulum deleuerit, consilium, auxilium aut assensum in aliquo premiissorum prebuerit, alienatum sit nomen eins de libro vite, & in hoc & in futuro seculo infirmitatem & damnacionem percipiat sempiternam. insuper & ipse & omnes fautores eius anathema sint maranatha. Fiat fiat in hijs scriptis. Amen.

This particularly thorough book curse spans over two folios at the beginning of a manuscript dating from the second half of the fourteenth century. The manuscript contains Augustine's commentary on the Psalms and belonged to the church now known as Titchfield Abbey. The Abbey was home to a community of Premonstratensian canons (also known as White Canons, after the colour of their habit), an austere order focused on prayer and study, but who also ministered to the laity. The severity of this order is reflected in their unyielding anathema, which makes sure to detail the different ways in which an individual might trigger the curse, and ensures that they suffer in this life as well as the next.

THE BOOK CURSE OF
WILLIAM WYMONDHAM

May he fare ill, wherever he goes,
That leaves this book to friend or to foe.
Amen.

Yll mowth he spede: where that he go,
That leuyth this boke: to frende or to foo.
Amen.

This hellish curse is written in a fifteenth-century miscellany that includes a range of texts on esoteric philosophy, chiromancy (palm reading), historical and medical notes, poems and prayers. The name William Wymondham, who was both the manuscript's scribe and its owner, is inscribed twice in the manuscript: he was part of the small community of Augustinian friars at the Priory of Kirby Bellars in Leicestershire. The book was clearly treasured by Wymondham: he writes in one note that he would rather lose all his worldly possessions than this book. The bookish malediction is written in red ink at the top of two consecutive folios, and its blood-like hue is both arresting and threatening.

POOKEFART'S BOOK CURSE

He who steals this book,
Shall be hanged upon a crook.
He who steal this book would,
May his heart quickly grow cold.
That it may be so, say amen, for devotion.
He who wrote the poem, 'Pookefart' is his name,
'Miller' is joined to it; that is what the writer is called.

He þat stelys this booke,
shulbe hanged on a crooke.
He that this booke stelle wolde,
sone be his herte colde.
That it mow so be, seiþ amen, for cherite.
Qui scripsit carmen, Pookefart est sibi nomen,
Miller jingatur qui scripsit sic nominator.

This jaunty book curse is found at the back of a fifteenth-century collection of sermons underneath another erased ownership inscription. The inscriber of this curse appears to have been called Miller, but uses the playful epithet Pookefart – perhaps to poke fun at the other ownership inscriptions in the manuscript, which were invariably penned by church rectors. The name 'Pookefart' translates into Modern English as 'Devil Fart' or 'Goblin Fart', and the name was often attached to a sprite-like character associated with mischief in Middle English poetic verse and folk wisdom. The first part of the name, 'pooke', is later used by Shakespeare for the character Puck in *A Midsummer Night's Dream*.

WILLIAM BENTLEY'S BOOK CURSE
INVOKING THE VIRGIN MARY

He who steals this book,
May Our Lady give him ill health.
Either with rope, sword or knife;
He shall have a short life.
Therefore, for the love of Our Lady,
I pray you let this book lie.
Said William Bentley.

He that thys boke dothe stele,
Oure lady yeff hym an euyll hele.
Othyr with rope, swerd or knyff;
he schall haue a schort lyfe.
þerfore, for þe love of oure lady,
I pray ȝou lett þis boke ly.
quod Wyllm Bentelee.

This book curse appears in a fifteenth-century manuscript which contains a lengthy history of England, known as the *Brut Chronical,* as well as tables on the solar and lunar eclipses. William Bentley writes the book curse twice on consecutive folios. Maybe he was attempting to impress its seriousness on the reader, or simply to practise his handwriting, as the curse is surrounded by pen trials of the alphabet and capital letters.

A BOOK CURSE
INSCRIBED IN A CHAINED BOOK

This book, legible in scripture,
Is here in this place attached with a chain,
So that it may endure,
And here perpetually still to remain,
From year to year; wherefore, upon pain
Of Christ's curse, of fathers and of mothers,
No one should hence attempt to remove it,
While any page rightly hangs with the others.

This present book legeble in scripture,
Here in this place thus tacched with a cheyn,
Purposed of entent for to endure,
And here perpetuelli stylle to remeyne,
Fro eyre to eyre; wherefore, appone peyn
Of cryst-is curs, of fadres and of moderes,
Non of hem hens attempt it to dereyne,
Whille any leef may goodeli hange with oder.

This book curse is written in a richly illustrated fifteenth-century manuscript known as The Rushall Psalter. While mainly consisting of liturgical texts, it also contains copies of two short poems by Geoffrey Chaucer, *Truth* and *Gentilesse*, some of Lydgate's poetic verses, and texts on living and dying well, which have been bound to the front of the manuscript.

This book curse, inscribed by the manuscript's original owner John Harpur of Rushall, is part of a longer poem. In a later verse it generously offers a pardon to anyone who repairs the book. The Rushall Psalter still bears is original iron chain, which would have secured the book to its bookcase (a common form of book protection in medieval European libraries), making this book curse a double protection against theft.

A BOOK CURSE THAT THREATENS
HANGING IN TWO WAYS

If any person steals this book,
He shall be hanged upon a hook.
Or by the neck with a rope.

If ony persone stele þis boke,
he shalbe hongyd by a hoke.
Or by the necke with a rope.

This book curse is inscribed in a fifteenth-century manuscript that principally contains *A Myrour to Lewde Men and Wymmen*, a prose version of the anonymous poem *Speculum Vitae*, which offers advice on how the laity can live devoutly. While the first two lines of the curse are written in red ink, the final line was added in black ink by a later hand, perhaps by someone who thought that the curse's threat needed to specify that the thief would indeed die from the punishment. The manuscript is peppered with other ownership inscriptions from both men and women from the fifteenth, sixteenth and seventeenth centuries.

JOHN HANCOK'S BOOK CURSE

This is John Hancok's book and whoever says nay,
The devil of hell bear Thomas Carter away!
Know before you knit, and then you may loosen it,
If you knit before you know, then it is too late.

Thys ys John hancok ys boke hoso euer saye naye,
the deuyll of hell bere Thomas carter awaye!
Know er thow knyt and then thow mayst slake,
Yf thow kynt er thow know then hyt ys to late.

This riddle-like curse features in a fifteenth-century manuscript that contains a collection of writings by Thomas Hoccleve. Hoccleve is often credited with writing the first autobiographical account of mental illness in the English language in his *Complaint*, which forms part of his wider work known as the *Series*. The poems are penned in Hoccleve's own hand, and the book was intended as a presentation copy – a gift – for Joan Beaufort, Countess of Westmoreland and niece of Geoffrey Chaucer. The Thomas Carter and John Hancok mentioned in the curse appear to have been cheeky scribes and are responsible for several of the inscriptions in the manuscript: a few folios later Thomas writes 'Thomas you be a good scrivener', a somewhat debatable claim as his inscription is almost completely covered by a smudge of ink from his own writing. Some scholars have speculated that the inscription conversations between John and Thomas indicate a schoolboy rivalry. The reference to knitting can also be understood as a reference to marriage, with the curse warning that you should not marry someone that you do not know – presumably in all senses.

ELEANOR WORCESTER'S BOOK CURSE

This book is one,
And God's curse is another.
They that take the one,
God give them the other.

Thys boke ys one,
and godes kors ys anoder.
They that take the ton,
god gef them the toder.

This book curse sits on the back of a printed paper fragment of canon law that has been added to the front of this
otherwise parchment manuscript. The manuscript itself is a
palm-sized book of hours and was owned by Eleanor, Countess
of Worcester, who inscribes the book several times with her
name. The curse, which is written in the same hand as other
notes by Eleanor Worcester, is followed on a later page by a
more mild-mannered request for the book to be returned if
found: 'This book is mine, Eleanor Worcester, and if I have
lost it and you find it, I pray you heartily to be so kind that you
will take a little trouble to see my book brought home again.'

JOHN TWYCHENER'S BOOK CURSE

This is John Twychener's book.
He that steals this book,
He shall be hanged upon a hook,
That will make his neck break,
And that will make his neck hang awry.

John Twychener ys boke.
He that stellys thys booke,
he shall be hangid a pon a hoke,
that wyll macke ys necke to brake,
and that wyll macke ys neck awrye.

This fifteenth-century manuscript contains the *Boke of Noblesse*, a text written by William Worcester that encouraged the invasion of France by the King of England. The book was initially addressed to Henry VI, but his name has been crossed out and the first folio of the manuscript names Edward IV instead. Worcester was the secretary of Sir John Fastolf, a famous knight who fought in the Hundred Years' War, identified by many as an inspirational figure for Shakespeare's character Falstaff.

A MISSING BOOK CURSE

He who steals this book,
Shall be hanged upon a hook,
Behind the kitchen door.

He þat stellen this boke,
he shalbe hanked apon a hok,
Behend the Kechen dore.

The last sighting of this manuscript was at a Sotheby's auction on 10 December 1962, where it was sold to an unknown buyer. The catalogue description for the item states that the pleasingly domestic curse was inscribed on the flyleaf of a Sarum Missal.

JOHN AUDELAY'S BOOK CURSE

No man may take this book away,
Nor cut out any page, and I'll tell you why,
For it is sacrilege, sirs, I tell you!
He will be cursed in the deed, it is true!
If you would like a copy,
Ask my permission and you will have
To pray for him especially,
Who has made this book your souls to save.
John the Blind Audelay:
The first priest to the Lord Strange he was,
Of this chantry, here in this place,
He made this book by God's grace,
Deaf, sick, blind, as he lay.

No mon þis book he take away,
Ny kutt owte noo leef, y say forwhy,
For hit ys sacrelege, sirus, y ȝow say!
Beþ accursed in the dede truly!
Ȝef ȝe wil have ani copi,
Askus leeve & ȝe shul have,
To pray for hym specialy
That hyt made ȝour soules to save,
Ion the Blynde Awdelay.
The furst prest to the Lord Strange he was,
Of þys chauntré, here in þis place,
That made þis bok by Goddus grace,
Deeff, siek, blynde, as he lay.

71

This extended curse appears in an early-fifteenth-century anthology containing the works of the priest and poet John Audelay. Audelay was chaplain to Richard le Strange of Knockin in Shropshire, and we know from several allusions within his poems that he was severely disabled by the end of his life. Many of Audelay's carols have been set to music by composers such as Hubert Parry and John Rutter. The manuscript also contains a second book curse, written on a hawking engraving pasted to the back cover by one John Barker, but the conclusion of its threat is illegible.

A BOOK CURSE INVOKING
GOD, MARY AND ALL THE SAINTS

Remember that in the year of our lord 1408,
John Popham, knight of the county of Southampton,
obtained and freely donated this book to the Church
of South Chardford on the Feast of the Purification
of the Virgin Mary, for his soul, and those of his
benefactors, let all who look at this volume pray
most piously, and whoever steals this book let the
anathema of God, the Blessed Mary, and all the saints
touch him forever. Amen. Amen. Amen for charity.

Memorandum quod anno domini millesimo cccc viii,
Iohannes Popham miles de comitatu Southamtonie,
comparavit et libere donavit istum librum ecclesie
parochiali de Southchardeforthe in festo purificacionis
beate virginis Marie, pro anima eius suorumque
benefactorum omnes hoc volumen inspicientes deum
piissime exorent, et istum librum qui alienaverit anathema
dei beate Marie et omnium sanctorum ei contingat
imperpetuum. amen. amen. amen par charite.

This thorough book curse is written at the beginning of an
early-fifteenth-century manuscript that was gifted by Sir John
Popham to the Church of South Chardford in Hampshire.
Interestingly, the manuscript also includes a dedicatory note
that grants an indulgence (a lessening of the time spent in pur-
gatory) of forty days to whoever walks around the cemetery.

A BOOK CURSE IN A MANUSCRIPT OF CHAUCER'S *TROILUS AND CRISEYDE*

He who this book tears or steals,
God send him the black sickness of hell.

He that thys Boke rentt stelle,
God send hym sekenys svart of helle.

This bookish malediction is inscribed at the beginning of an early-fifteenth-century manuscript that contains one of the best copies of Geoffrey Chaucer's romance of *Troilus and Criseyde*. The elaborately illustrated frontispiece depicts Chaucer reading to members of the English court. The two-line curse is written on a folio which features the illustration on its verso, after another inscription in a different hand that reads: 'Lord God preserve under your mighty hands, the King, the Queen, the people of this land.' The Middle English adjective *svart* is generally used to describe something that is black, dark or clouded-over, but can also be used to describe something that is evil, wicked or angry.

AGNES LYELL'S BOOK CURSE

This book belongs to Mistress Agnes Lyell.
Whoever steals this book shall have
Christ's curse and mine.

Iste liber constat Domina Agnese Lye[ll].
Hoo thys boke stelyth schall have cryst curse and myne.

Agnes Lyell's book curse is written in a manuscript that contains the *Pore Catiff* (Poor Wretch), a manual of religious instruction for the laity. With this short book curse, Lyell manages to convey both her piety and her ferocious ownership over the book, promising the reader that, should they steal her tome, they would face the combined force of both herself and God. The curse is written on the final folio of the manuscript, on a page that is very dark and stained.

THE TWO BOOK CURSES OF
ST ALDATE'S CHURCH, GLOUCESTER

This book belongs to St Aldate.
This book is one and Christ's curse is another,
He that takes the one also takes the other. Amen.

Iste libert pertinet ad sanctum Aldatum.
Thys boke ys one and chryst curse ys Anoþer,
he þat take þe one take þe oþer Amen.

This book is of St Aldate.
He that steals the book shall be hauled by the neck.

Thys boke ys sancht Audatys.
He þat stelys þe boke shall be haulynth by þe neck.

These two book curses, both pertaining to the Church of St
Aldate in Gloucester, are found in a liturgical manual. The
church was badly damaged in the English Civil War, and
demolished in 1653.

THE TWO BOOK CURSES OF ST ALBANS STUDENTS ATTENDING GLOUCESTER COLLEGE, OXFORD

This book is given
for the use of the brothers at Oxford
By John Whethamstede, the father of the flock
of the proto-martyr of the English.
If anyone steals it, or viciously removes its inscription,
May he feel Judas' noose [around his neck]
and pitchforks [in hell]. Amen.

Fratribus Oxonie datur in munus liber iste
Per Johannem Whethamstede patrem
pecorum prothomartiris Amgligenarum.
quem si quis raptat raptim, titulumve retractet,
vel Iude laqueum vel furcas sensiat. amen.

This book curse is written at the beginning of a manuscript used by monks studying at Gloucester College, University of Oxford. The book belonged to the Benedictine community at St Albans Abbey during the abbacy of John Whethamstede, whose name appears in another anathema written later in the manuscript. Whethamstede built a significant library at St Albans, and many of the books that were owned by the abbey and shared with Gloucester College contain bookish maledictions. Whethamstede's skeleton was uncovered in 2017, and his face forensically reconstructed by a team at Liverpool John Moores University.

A BOOK CURSE THREATENING
DIFFERENT PUNISHMENTS
FOR THIEVING MEN AND
THIEVING WOMEN

God bless the hands of the writer at all times.
And whoever steals me will be hanged by the neck,
And if they are a woman burned in fire.

Manus scriptoris salvet deus omnibus horis.
Et qui furabitur per collum suspendatur,
Et si mulier in igne comburatur.

This unusual book curse is found towards the end of a
fifteenth-century manuscript that contains various saints' lives
and devotional poems. The execution methods of hanging and
burning at the stake were used in fifteenth-century Europe
to punish the most serious of crimes (such as the murder of
an employer by their employee, or the murder of a husband
by his wife) because such crimes were perceived as upsetting
the natural and divinely ordained social order. That this book
curse threatens the most severe of punishments is reflective
of the value of the book, and the curse-writer's belief that
thieves' deaths should work as a public deterrent to others
plotting to smuggle manuscripts.

THE BOOK CURSE OF
PETRUS LEO ORTINUS

Petrus Leo Ortinus wrote:
Who steals from me shall be hanged on three trees.
Praise be to God.

Petrus Leo Ortinus scripsit:
Qui me furatur in tribus lignis suspendatur.
Deo gratias.

This brief but effective bookish malediction is written in an
Italian manuscript, and helpfully dated to 1461. The manuscript
contains the Latin work *Strategemata* by the Roman civil engi-
neer and senator Frontinus, which offers a detailed description
of various military strategies from Roman and Greek history.
Petrus's reference to 'three trees' is an allusion to the gallows
that were often constructed from three trunks to create a
horizontal triangle, or two upright posts and a crossbeam.

A BOOK CURSE IN A
MUSIC BOOK FOR ROYALTY

He who steals this book,
Shall be hanged upon a hook,
Either by water or by land,
With a good hemp band.

He That stelle Thys boke,
A shalle be hangked vp on a hoke,
no vther be water nor be lond,
wyt a fayer hempyng bond.

This book curse is written in the front of a beautiful late-fifteenth-century or early-sixteenth-century manuscript that contains a range of polyphonic music and was intended for royalty. Book historians and musicologists debate whether the book was made for a member of the French or English royal family: a miniature which may have offered a clue as to who it was intended for has been cut out of the manuscript.

DOROTHY HELBARTON'S
BOOK CURSE

This is my mistress' book,
who ought to have him [the book],
Whoever would lock it away from her:
you are a true villain.

Thys my mystrys boke who outeyth hym for to haue,
Who so whoulde agenstey loke ye ys a vere knaue.

Dorothy Helbarton's book curse is written in a manuscript containing the Middle English *Brut* (a chronicle of the history of England), alongside a Latin prophesy and some medical recipes. It was this manuscript that was used by William Caxton as the exemplar from which he printed *The Chronicles of England*, and is the only exemplar of one of his English editions to survive. Several notes in the book tell us that this book was gifted to Helbarton by her mother, whose last name was Barnard. The manuscript contains over sixty inscriptions relating to Helbarton, and the handwriting of these notes is consistent with the styles of the early sixteenth century. These inscriptions seem to have be written by a male scribe, who in one note writes that 'he that will record this is my mistress' book'.

WILLIAM HOK'S
SKIN-ROTTING BOOK CURSE

William Hok owns this book,
And he that steals this book –
May the devil rot off his skin.

Wyllyam Hok oth thys bok,
and he that thys bok stels –
the dele rot off hys uels.

This particularly gruesome book curse is from a fifteenth-century book of hours. The curse itself is written in a sixteenth-century hand, and its context is somewhat confusing: below the curse, the same hand writes that 'William Hok gave me this book', perhaps indicating that the book was passed between a father and son with the same name. Clearly, the effects of the bookish malediction were feared enough for this second confirmatory note to have been penned. The disturbing threat that the book thief's skin will rot off is perhaps reflective of the symptoms of leprosy, which caused lesions to open on the skin and which could lead to the loss of the fingers, toes and nose.

HUGH OF WOLLASTON'S
BOOK CURSE

This book belongs to Hugh of Wollaston.
Whoever steals it: let him be anathema.
Whoever finds fault with these poems:
let him be cursed. Amen.

Iste liber constat Hugoni de Wolaston.
Quicunque alienaverit anathema sit.
Qui culpat carmen sit maledictus. Amen.

This book curse, which curses anyone who criticizes the
metrical version of the Psalms which it contains (translated
from Latin to Middle English), was written in the sixteenth
century.

EARLY MODERN BOOK CURSES

THE EARLY MODERN PERIOD SAW THE HISTORICAL EVENTS of the English Renaissance, Reformation and Enlightenment, and great leaps in the development of the technology used to make books. The invention of the moveable-type printing press by Johannes Gutenberg in the 1440s gradually revolutionized the way that people made, consumed and understood books as objects. Some of the earlier bookish maledictions found in this chapter are written in late-medieval manuscripts that were still bought and sold while printing was slowly being adopted, and others are written in 'incunabula' – books printed before 1500.

Printing enabled books to be produced more quickly and, when the technology became widespread and commonplace, more cheaply too. It also contributed to a rise in literacy rates, as printed media became more widely available and books were often printed in the vernacular

– the language spoken by ordinary people. The proliferation of different media, like broadsheets (a single sheet, cheaply produced, that could feature a ballad or news, sometimes illustrated) and chapbooks (small publications of shorter texts, often accompanied by woodcut illustrations), meant people's literacy could be supported by visual aids, or be used to follow performances. The printed word was also harnessed to effect religious and political change, as new ideas were spread through clandestine networks, or published to wider audiences in order to incite action. Kings and commoners alike used print media to consolidate their power and increase support for their various causes, and ownership of particular books or pamphlets could lead to incarceration and execution.

The kind of books that bear curses in this period remain varied. In this chapter you will find curses written in books of culinary recipes, as well as those of philosophy and practical sciences. This period also welcomes the first book curses definitely penned by children, whose age does not stop them from threatening punishments just as brutal as those inscribed by readers of more mature years. This is reflective of the increase in children's literature published in the 1700s, which rapidly increased in number and creativity through the latter half of the century. These book curses also introduce the threat of social dishonour, and many of the later curses deter would-be book pilferers by inciting a 'fear of shame'.

AN EARLY MODERN BOOK CURSE WRITTEN IN A LATE MEDIEVAL MANUSCRIPT

Your master's book does scorn your name,
To scribble therein, then cease for shame.
John Weeks.

Thy masters booke dothe scorne thy name,
To scrible therein then cease for shame.
Iohannem Wekes.

This late-sixteenth-century book curse is written in a fifteenth-century manuscript containing Geoffrey Chaucer's *Canterbury Tales*. Underneath this rhyming couplet is another note in a different hand that responds to the curse:

My masters booke will geve me lefe
too scribble therin y ask no lefe.

This is a play on words: *lefe* can be understood as either the leaf of a manuscript or to give permission – to grant 'leave'.

THE UNIVERSITY OF
CAMBRIDGE BOOK CURSE

Whoever spoils me by treating me badly
or steals me from the University:
let him be anathema, unless he make amends.

qui male tractando me spoliaverit
uel ab academia alienaverit
anathema sit, nisi emendauerit.

This book curse features on the title page of the *Liber privilegi-orum et libertatum alme universitatis Cantebrigiensis,* a manuscript containing transcriptions of important documents concerning the privileges granted to the University of Cambridge. The documents were transcribed by the professional scribe Robert Hare, who worked as Clerk of the Pells (a role in the Exchequer responsible for logging receipts and payments on rolls of parchment called 'pells', after the Latin word for skin or hide: *pellis*). This role evidently gave Hare plenty of time to perfect the neat script with which he transcribes the documents and in which he writes this bookish malediction, which sits on the title page of the manuscript.

A SCOTS BOOK CURSE WRITTEN IN AN INCUNABULUM

This book belongs to Lord Ogilvy of
Dunlugas, Knight. With joy, without pain.
He that steals this book from me,
God grant that he is hanged on a tree,
Amen for me, Amen for thee,
Amen for all good company.
Witness with your own hand.

Iste liber pertinet ad dominum galterum ogilvy de
dunlugus, Milite. Cum gaudio absque dolore.
he yat stelis us Buyk fra me,
god gif he be hangit one ane tre,
amen for me, amen for the,
amen for all gud cumpani.
Teste manu propria.

This book curse is written in an incunabulum printed in 1474 in Leuven, Belgium. The book contains an adapted version of *Historia Alexandri Magni* (*The History of Alexander the Great*), the *Gesta Romanorum* (*The Deeds of the Romans*), and the *Consolatio peccatorum* (about a legal trial between Christ and Satan). Another inscription indicates that the treasured tome was passed down from Sir Walter Ogilvy to his son George Ogilvy, First Lord of Banff, a Scottish Royalist army officer. The Latin phrase *manu propria*, 'signed with one's own hand', was often used on official documents instead of, or alongside, a signature and is perhaps employed here to lend authority to the curse.

JOHN BARCLAY'S BOOK CURSE, WRITTEN IN A MEDICAL BOOK

John Barcllay This booke is mine
he that steles this booke frome me
shaal be hanged on a tre

John Barclay's book curse is written in a printed book containing a volume on philosophy and medicine by the late-medieval Swiss writer Paracelsus, who is credited with being the father of toxicology (the study, diagnosing and treatment of toxins and toxicants). His work was translated by the English apothecary John Hester, and printed in 1580. Bound with this book is another volume on how to diagnose illnesses from observing human urine.

A BOOK CURSE WITH THE
NAME SCRATCHED OUT

… his book, Amen.
And he that this book does steal,
Shall be hanged in gaol. 1644.

… his booke Amen.
And hee that douth this bouke stayll,
hee shall be hanged at gaylle. 1644.

This bookish malediction is found on the final page of a
printed edition of Thomas Blundell's *Exercises*, published in
1613. Blundell was an English humanist writer, keen equestrian
and mathematics tutor to some of the great English families
of the late sixteenth century. The book is a collection of six
treaties on various practical sciences and describes itself as
'very necessarie to be read and learned of all young gentlemen'. Such necessary reading includes instructions on how to
use an astrolabe, details on cosmography (the features of the
universe) and tips for navigation. The inscriber of the book
curse has had their name expunged, perhaps by a later owner
who wanted to remove evidence of their theft, but the efficacy
of the malediction is retained.

ROBERT HERRICK'S 'TO MOMUS'

> Who read'st this Book that I have writ,
> And can'st not mend, but carpe at it:
> By all the muses! thou shalt be
> Anathema to it, and me.

This book-curse-like poem by Robert Herrick is titled 'To Momus', after the mythological Greek god of satire and 'carping' (fault-finding) criticism Momus, who was often invoked in seventeenth-century literature. Herrick was a poet and Anglican cleric who wrote a prodigious amount of verse in his lifetime. 'To Momus' features in his collection *Hesperides*, which contains over one thousand poems. Another poem in the collection is an amusing warning against using the pages of the book as toilet paper:

> Who with thy leaves shall wipe (at need)
> The place, where swelling Piles do breed:
> May every Ill, that bites, or smarts,
> Perplexe him in his hinder-parts.

JEAN GEMEL'S BOOK CURSE

Jean Gembel her book,
I wish she may be drouned that
Steals it from her.

This short book curse is found in a book of recipes dating
from between 1660 and 1700. The manuscript contains over
ninety recipes, most of which are culinary, but some of which
are medicinal or relating to household management. Many
of the culinary recipes are for fruit preserves, but there are
plenty concerning other foods which would have been served
at banquets. The owner of the book was a woman named
Jean Gemel, who spells her name *Gemel*, *Gembel* and *Gemmell*
at different points in the manuscript. This book curse is not
found at the beginning or end of the manuscript, but at the
bottom of a page with recipes 'To make orange pudding' and
'For making venison of mutton'.

GERARD COOPER'S BOOK CURSE

Gerard Cooper his Book,
God give him grace therein to look.
Not only look, but Understand,
For Learning is better than House & Land.
When House & Land is gone & spent,
Then Learning is most excellent.
Steal not this Book, my honest Friend,
For fear the Gallows will be your end.
Steal not this Book for fear of Shame,
For underneath stands the owner's Name.
Gerard Cooper his Book
November the 4th, 1704

Gerard Cooper's book curse is written in the front of a 1616 copy of Erasmus' *Adagiorum*, a collection of annotated Greek and Latin proverbs.

MARY FEARMAN'S BOOK CURSE, WRITTEN IN A BOOK OF FAIRY TALES

Mary Fearman
Her Book God give her grace unto
Look not to look but understand
Learning is better than house or land,
Steal not this Book for fear of shame
For hear you'll find
The <u>owners</u> name
December 18 1742

This emphatic book curse was inscribed in a 3rd-edition copy of Charles Perrault's *Histories, or Tales of Passed Times,* printed in London in 1741. The collection is also known as *The Tales of Mother Goose* and includes the well-known tales of 'Little Red Riding Hood', 'Puss in Boots' and 'Cinderella'. Fearman was clearly proud of her book; her inscription is neatly written in black pen, and she underlined the word 'owners' to emphasize her possession over the volume (and, perhaps, to point the reader back to her own fairy-tale villain-esque surname). While the rhyming couplets of the curse could have been more fully emphasized if Fearman had placed them at the end of her lines, her more individualized lineation adds a rakish charm to the malediction.

ELIZABETH PARSONS' BOOK CURSE

Elizabeth Parsons, her book, 1774.
Those who steal this book:
Send them straight
To the pearly gates.

Elizabeth Parsons Her Book, 1774.
Them that doth this Book stale:
Will send them staight
To perly gaate.

Elizabeth Parsons' book curse is written in a printed school-book produced as part of the 'Reformation of Manners', a Protestant movement that aimed to increase literacy, improve scriptural knowledge and condemn Catholic practices. The book itself was printed in 1707, and contains some rather grue-some woodcuts of important historical events, including the Great Fire of London, the Gunpowder Plot and the torture of Protestants under Queen Mary. The book curse is written on a blank page that sits opposite an acrostic alphabet poem, and perhaps Elizabeth took inspiration for her curse from the lines beginning with N: 'Never revenge thy self; for God will pay, / Thy Adversaries off another Day.'

A CURSE IN A BOOK OF
CHEMISTRY LECTURES

Whoever thrusts their fingernails into this book
and does not return it to its master:
go to the black underworld.

si quis in hunc librum vapidos injecerit ungues
ni reddat domino tartara nigra petat

This bookish malediction is written in a manuscript containing the chemistry lectures given by John Mickleburgh at the University of Cambridge in the first half of the eighteenth century. Mickleburgh uses the distinctive phrase *tartara nigra*, referring to Tartarus, the deep abyss of judgement and punishment that features in Greek mythology.

HENRY PIGOT'S BOOK CURSE

This book is mine, and none of thine,
therefore let it alone.
If you take it I will brake your pate
and send you home.

Henry Pigot's rhyming book curse is written on the flyleaf of *Christmas Tales for the Amusement and Instruction of Young Ladies and Gentlemen in Winter Evenings*. The book contains a variety of fantastical tales along with detailed woodcut illustrations. The author of the book is named as one 'Solomon Sobersides', a pseudonym befitting the moralistic and didactic content of the book. No printing date is given, but various editions of the book are dated from the mid-eighteenth century to the early nineteenth century.

Modern
BOOK CURSES

At the start of the nineteenth century, books were still being made using techniques and materials similar to those of the sixteenth. This quickly began to change as a blizzard of technological developments impacted every part of the book-making process, from paper production to cover design. In the late twentieth century, the dawn of the internet age altered book consumption and distribution even more: internet-based bookstores could post books around the world, and readers could access thousands of titles from screens that weighed less than a paperback. These later advances, however, did not unravel readers' attachment to their material texts: many bibliophiles will tell you that there is nothing like the smell of a new book, or the feeling of turning over its pages for the first time.

As in the previous chapter, several of the bookish maledictions found here are penned by child cursers. Indeed, the association between children and book curses becomes so strong that young readers are often depicted as writing curses within fictional tales, and a couple of the most

notable can be found here. Many of the bookish maledictions of the nineteenth and twentieth centuries are found
on bookplates – labels that are pasted into a book (usually
its inside cover). These plates usually feature the name of
the book's owner and saved them from writing out their
details by hand. The bookplate curses in this chapter
belonged to a diverse range of book collectors, from those
noted for their impressive collection of fishing books to
those of a cowboy actor. Bookplates commonly feature
designs relating to the identity of the book's owner, and
later bookplates often humorously incorporate elements
of their work and life into their design, alongside some
comically threatening curses.

JOHN CLARE'S BOOK CURSE

Steal not this book for fear of Shame
For here doth Stand the owners Name.
John Clare
1806

John Clare is widely regarded as one of the greatest English poets, best known for his poetic works on rural life and nature. This bookish malediction is inscribed on the cover of one of Clare's old school exercise books and was written when he was thirteen years old, just two years after he had completed his formal education.

DAVID H. HOOPER'S
BRAIN-BEATING BOOK CURSE

Don't steal this
Book if you do I will
Beat your Brains
Out

This book curse was penned by one David H. Hooper in a copy of Noah Webster's *The American Spelling Book*, published in 1819. *The American Spelling Book*, also known as the 'Blue-Backed Speller' because of its distinctive blue cover, was extremely popular, and was one of the first spelling books to present American spelling as distinct from that of British English. Hooper signs his name after the curse, and the reader is left to wonder if he planned on beating the thief's brain out with his fists, or with the book itself.

MARY LUCRETIA SHELTON'S
BOOK CURSE

Steal not this Book my honest
friend for fear the gallows will
be your end For god will say in
the judgement day where
is that Book you stole away
Mary Lucretia Sheltons Book
Labour for Learning Before
you grow old Learning is
better than silver or gold

Mary Lucretia Shelton inscribed her book curse twice in her 1816 copy of Lindley Marray's *Introduction to the English Reader*, once on the front flyleaf, and again on the back flyleaf (where it is written upside down). Murray's anthologies were popular at the start of the nineteenth century and contained a range of poetry and prose to aid memorization, reading aloud and a general familiarity with the literary canon of the time. The two book curses are dated to 1821. Like some other examples written by young cursers, Shelton's unusual lineation disrupts the reader's expectation of rhyme and contributes to the curse's unsettling effect.

A NEWGATE GAOL BOOK CURSE

<u>Caution</u>

Steal not this Book my honest friend,
or else the Gallows will be your end
And if I catch you by the Tail,
I will lodge you safe in Newgate Gaol;
and when the Judge will come to say
where is that Book you have stolen away,
and if you say you do not know,
he will say go down below.

dated 1865

This mid-nineteenth-century book curse is inscribed in a collection of almanacs that have been bound together, dating from 1776 to 1790. Almanacs were a popular kind of print medium in the eighteenth century, and often included the dates for important anniversaries, political events and meteorological and astronomical happenings. This book curse makes reference to London's Newgate Gaol at an interesting point in the history of prison reform. In the late eighteenth century, Newgate Gaol replaced the Tyburn gallows as London's foremost stage for public hangings, and the execution of notorious murderers could draw crowds of thousands, sometimes causing crushes. The last public hanging at Newgate took place in 1868, just three years after this curse was penned.

EDMUND LESTER PEARSON'S
HOAX BOOK CURSE

For him that stealeth a Book from this Library,
let it change to a Serpent in his hand and rend him.
Let him be struck with Palsy, and all his Members
blasted. Let him languish in Pain, crying aloud for
Mercy and let there be no surcease to his Agony till
he sink to Dissolution. Let Book-worms gnaw his
Entrails in token of the Worm that dieth not, and
when at last he goeth to his final Punishment let
the Flames of Hell consume him for ever and aye.

This protracted bookish malediction features in *The Old Librarian's Almanack*, which was published in 1909 and written by Edmund Lester Pearson, an American librarian and crime fiction author. *The Almanack* is a humorous book that masquerades as 'A very rare pamphlet first published in New Haven Connecticut in 1773'. This curse was supposedly discovered in the non-existent San Pedro monastery in Barcelona by the fictitious Sir Matthew Mahan, who then translated it from Latin into English. Pearson was evidently well versed in book-curse tropes, and his hoax of a curse is often mistaken for a real bookish malediction.

C.J. PEACOCK'S BOOKPLATE CURSE

From the library of C.J. Peacock.
Whoever folds a page down,
The devil toast brown.
Who makes a mark or a blot,
The devil roast hot.
Whoever steals this book,
The devil will cook.

C.J. Peacock Ex Libris.
Who folds a leafe downe
Ye diuel toaste browne,
Who make marke or blotte
Ye diuel roaste hot,
Who stealeth thiße boke
Ye diuel shall cooke.

This faux-medieval bookplate was that of C.J. Peacock, a book collector who operated from Tunbridge Wells. The bookplate design features Peacock's initials in the shape of a strutting peacock, and the book curse appears in faux-Gothic print in a scroll at the bottom. Its concern with the devil and fire echoes some of the medieval book curses featured earlier in this volume.

JENNY'S JOURNAL BOOK
CURSE IN *CROME YELLOW*

Black is the raven, black is the rook,
But blacker the thief who steals this book!

This book curse is penned by Jenny Mullion, a partially deaf
character in Aldous Huxley's satirical novel *Crome Yellow*,
published in 1921. The curse is discovered by the protagonist
Denis, who snoops through Jenny's private journal only to find
cutting caricatures of himself and the other guests he is staying
with for the summer.

FRANK BARKER'S BOOK CURSE
IN *EMILY OF NEW MOON*

Steal not this book for fear of shame
For on it is the owners [*sic*] name
And when you die the Lord will say
Where is the book you stole away
And when you say you do not know
The Lord will say go down below

This bookish malediction is penned by Frank Barker, an antagonistic character in Lucy Maud Montgomery's novel *Emily of New Moon*, which was first published in 1923. Montgomery is perhaps better known for her *Anne of Green Gables* series, and the adventures of orphan Emily likewise centre around a community on Prince Edward Island. Frank writes the rhymed book curse on the front page of Emily's new reader; she subsequently rips out the page and burns it.

A COWBOY'S BOOKPLATE CURSE

The Good Book Says
'God Helps Those That Help Themselves.'
But I Say 'God Help The Man
That Strays Off The Ranch With This Book.'

This bookplate curse was used by Thomas Edwin Mix (better known as Tom Mix), an American movie star who helped define the Western film genre, and who was referred to as the 'King of Cowboys'. His bookplate is rendered to look like a brown raw cow hide, with the text written in a darker brown as if it had been branded into the skin – it appears to threaten the book thief with a similar branding if caught.

MALCOLM M. FERGUSON'S
BOOKPLATE CURSE

Ex Libris
Malcolm M. Ferguson
To him who sends a stealing hand
And it comes not back at his command
Send not the other – you can yet
Borrow the book – and then forget.

This foreboding book curse was used in the bookplate of the author Malcolm M. Ferguson, who was known for his works of Weird Fiction, a genre of fiction which combines elements of horror, the supernatural and fantasy. The bookplate features an illustration of a bony hand that has been stabbed by a dagger decorated with archaic symbols as it reaches for the spines of books bearing titles like *Necronomicon* and *Horrid Rites*.

JOHN SIMPSON'S BOOKPLATE CURSE

John Simpson
Owns this book
If it you should hook
May God choke you.
Eaton: 1981.

John Sympson
Oweth thyse booke
Yf it ye shde hooke
May God ye Chooke.
Eaton: M.CM.lxxxi.

This bookish malediction was devised by John Simpson, a collector of bookplates and books on fishing. Simpson's bookplate uses a faux-Middle English curse, and features an illustration of a man in late medieval dress fishing on a river in the foreground, whilst the ghost of a hanged man is embraced by the arms of a black devil in the background. At the top of the bookplate a godly hand points to the executed sinner, and a banderole pronounces that 'He Stole John's Booke'.

SELECT
BIBLIOGRAPHY

Bale, Anthony, 'Belligerent Literacy, Bookplates and Graffiti: Dorothy Helbarton's Book', in *Book Destruction from the Medieval to the Contemporary*, ed. Gill Partington and Adam Smyth (London: Macmillan, 2014), pp. 89–112.

Casson, Lionel, *Libraries in the Ancient World* (New Haven CT: Yale University Press, 2001).

Crain, Patricia, *Reading Children: Literacy, Property, and the Dilemmas of Childhood in Nineteenth-Century America* (Philadelphia PA: University of Pennsylvania Press, 2016).

Drieshen, Clarck, 'Frying pans, forks and fever: Medieval book curses', British Library Medieval Manuscripts Blog, https://blogs.bl.uk/digitisedmanuscripts/2017/05/frying-pans-forks-and-fever-medieval-book-curses.html (accessed 13 October 2023).

Drogin, Mark, *Anathema! Medieval Scribes and the History of Book Curses* (Montclair NJ: Allanheld & Schram, 1983).

Gameson, Richard, '"Signed" Manuscripts in Early Romanesque Flanders: Saint-Bertin and Saint Vaast', in *Pen in Hand: Medieval Scribal Portraits, Colophons and Tools*, ed. Michael Gullick (Walkern: Red Gull Press, 2006), pp. 31–74.

Ingram, Randall, 'Robert Herrick and the Making of *Hersperides*', *Studies in English Literature* 38 (1998), pp. 127–47.

Jackson, Hollbrook, *The Anatomy of Bibliomania*, vol. II (London: Soncino Press, 1931).

Northall, G.F., *English Folk-Rhymes: A Collection of Traditional Verses Relating to Places and Persons, Customs, Superstitions* (London: Kegan Paul, 1892).

O'Hagan, Lauren Alex, 'Steal not this book my honest friend: Threats, Warnings, and Curses in the Edwardian Book', *Textual Cultures: Text, Contexts, Interpretation* 13 (2020), pp. 244–74.

Sheridan, Dana, 'Cursed Books', Princeton University Cotsen Children's Library Pop Goes the Page Blog, https://popgoesthepage.princeton.edu/book-curses (accessed 13 October 2023).

Taylor, Jon, Enrique Jiménez, Babette Schnitzlein and Sophie Cohen, 'The Colophons of Ashurbanipal, King of the World', in *Literary Snippets: Colophons Across Space and Time*, ed. George A. Kiraz and Sabine Schmidtke (Athens GA: Georgias Press, 2023), pp. 23–42.

Whitelock, Dorothy, *English Historical Documents*, Volume I: *c. 500-1042* (London: Routledge, 1996).

Wingfield, Emily, 'Ex libris domini duncani/ Cambell de glenwrquhay/ miles': *The Buik of King Alexander the Conqueror* in the household of Sir Duncan Campbell, seventh laird of Glenorchy', in *Medieval Romance, Medieval Contexts*, ed. Rhiannon Purdie and Michael Cichon (Woodbridge: D.S. Brewer, 2011), pp. 161–74.

SOURCES

BOOK CURSES FROM ANTIQUITY

The curse of Yahdun-Lim's temple dedication
Paris, Louvre Museum, Département des Antiquités orientales, AO 21815. Translation from A. Leo Oppenheim, 'Assyrian and Babylonian Historical Texts', in *The Ancient Near East: An Anthology of Texts and Pictures,* ed. James B. Pritchard (Princeton NJ: Princeton University Press, 2011), pp. 247–8.

The curse of Ḥammurabi's law stele
Paris, Louvre Museum, Richelieu Wing, Room 227. Translation from Kathryn Slanski, *Entitlement Narus: A Study in Form and Function* (Boston MA: American Schools of Oriental Research, 2003), p. 263.

The curse of a Sefire treaty stele
Syria, National Museum of Damascus, Stele I (face C, inscription 9). Translation from Joseph A. Fitzmyer, *The Aramaic Inscriptions of Sefire* (Rome: Editrice Pontificio Istituto Biblico, 1995), p. 55.

The curse of Shalmaneser IV's commemoration stele
Istanbul, Archaeological Museum of Istanbul, Inventory no. 1326. Translation from Sandra L. Richter, *The Deuteronomistic History and the Name Theology: leshakken shemo sham in the Bible and the Ancient Near East* (Berlin: De Gruyter, 2014), p. 135.

The curse of Sargon II's memorial stele
Berlin, Pergamon Museum (Vorderasiatisches Museum),

Reference no. VA 00968. Translation from Daniel David Lucken-
bill, *Ancient Records of Assyria and Babylonia* (Chicago IL: Chicago
University Press, 1927), p. 45.

A curse from the library of Ashurbanipal
London, British Museum (Ashurbanipal Library Colophon e,
BAK319). Translation from 'Ashurbanipal Library Colophon e' by the
project *Reading the Library of Ashurbanipal: A multi-sectional Analysis
of Assyriology's Foundational Corpus (RLBsa)*, British Museum and
Ludwig Maximilian University Munich, oracc.museum.upenn.edu/
asbp/rlasb/pager.

EARLY MEDIEVAL BOOK CURSES

The curse of Bishop Ælfsiga's will
Oxfordshire, Shirburn Castle, MS. Liber Monasterii de Hyda, f. 19r.

The curse of King Æthelred's land grant
London, British Library, Cotton MS. Claudius B VI, ff. 96r–97r.

Constantius' book curse
Bern, Burgerbibliothek, Cod. 87 (f. 17v).

The Latin and Old English book curse of Bishop Leofric of Exeter
Oxford, Bodleian Library, MS. Auct. F. 3. 6, f. 3v.

A book curse threatening hell's possession
Boulogne, Bibliothèque municipale des Annonciades, MS. 20, f. 1r.

A book curse blessing scribes and pushing thieves into hell
Arras, Médiathèque de l'Abbaye Saint-Vaast, MS. 732/CGM 684, f. 131r.

A book curse comparing Christ's body to a manuscript page
Arras, Médiathèque de l'Abbaye Saint-Vaast, MS. 860/ CGM 530 (f. 1r).

HIGH MEDIEVAL BOOK CURSES

A book curse repeated every year by candlelight
London, British Library, Harley MS. 3061 (f. 1r).

Abbot Simon's book curse
Cambridge, Trinity Hall, MS. 2 (f. 1v).

The book curse of the Abbey of Saints Mary & Nicholas, Arnstein
London, British Library, MS. Harley 2798 (f. 235v).

The book curse of Santa Maria della Colomba
New Haven CT, Yale University, Beinecke Rare Book and Manuscript Library, Takamiya MS. 125 (recto).

The book curse of the Abbey of Mont-Saint-Quentin
New Haven CT, Yale University, Beinecke Rare Book and
Manuscript Library, Beinecke MS. 214 (f. 1r).
The year-long book curse of Rochester Priory
London, British Library, Royal MS. 12 G II (f. 1v).
The book curse of Robert of Aldsworth
Cambridge, Corpus Christi College, MS. 485 (front inside binding).
The book curse of the Ancrene Wisse
Cambridge, Corpus Christi College, MS. 402 (f. 1r).
Cambridge, St John's College, MS. H.11.
The curse of the Abbey of St Mary the Virgin, Robertsbridge
Oxford, Bodleian Library, MS. Bodl. 132 (fol. 228r).
A simple book curse threatening hanging
London, British Library, Additional MS. 40675 (f. 3r).
A book curse praising scribes and damning thieves
Paris, Bibliothèque nationale de France, MS. Latin 3278 (f. 383r).
The book curse of Newark Priory
Oxford, Bodleian Library, MS. Laud Misc. 548 (f. 3r).

LATE MEDIEVAL BOOK CURSES

A book curse in a manuscript containing volvelles
Cambridge, Corpus Christi College, MS. 037 (f. 1v).
John Wryghtson's book curse
Oxford, St John's College, MS. 76 (f. 4v).
The Gonville & Caius College book curse
Cambridge, Gonville & Caius College, MS. 394/614 (f. 211r).
*A book curse threatening illness in this life and eternal damnation in
the next* Oxford, Bodleian Library, MS. Bodl. 249 (ff. 2v–3r).
The book curse of William Wymondham
Cambridge, Trinity College, MS. O.2.40 (ff. 51v–52r).
Pookefart's book curse
London, British Library, Royal MS. 18 A XVII (f. 199r).
William Bentley's book curse invoking the Virgin Mary
London, Lambeth Palace Library, MS. 259 (f. 4r).
A book curse inscribed in a chained book
Nottingham, Nottingham University Library, Mellish Lm 1
(f. 20v).

A book curse that threatens hanging in two ways
 London, British Library, Harley MS 45 (f. 169r).
John Hancok's book curse
 Durham, Durham University Library, MS. Cosin V.iii.9 (f. 37v).
Eleanor Worcester's book curse
 London, British Library, MS. 1251 (f. 1r).
John Twychener's book curse
 London, British Library, Royal MS. 18 B XXII (f. 42v).
John Audelay's book curse
 Oxford, Bodleian Library, MS. Douce 302 (f. 35r).
A book curse invoking God, Mary, and all the saints
 London, British Library, Royal MS. 2 A XXI (f. 2v).
A book curse in a manuscript of Chaucer's Troilus and Criseyde
 Cambridge, Corpus Christi College, MS. 61 (f. 1r).
The two book curses of St Aldate's Church, Gloucester
 London, British Library, Additional MS. 30506 (ff. 169r, 170r).
The two book curses of St Albans students attending Gloucester College,
 Oxford London, British Library, Royal MS. 8 G X (f. 1v).
A book curse threatening different punishments for thieving men and
 thieving women Paris, Bibliotèque nationale de France, MS. 24954
 (p. 217).
The book curse of Petrus Leo Ortinus
 London, British Library, Burney MS. 173 (f. 76v).
A book curse in a music book for royalty
 Cambridge, Magdalene College, Pepys MS. 1760 (front pastedown).
Dorothy Helbarton's book curse
 San Marino CA, The Huntington Library, MS. HM 136 (f. 80r).
William Hok's skin-rotting book curse
 London, British Library, Harley MS. 1845 (f. 8v).
Hugh of Wollaston's book curse
 Oxford, Bodleian Library, MS. Bodl. 921 (f. 99v).

EARLY MODERN BOOK CURSES

An early modern book curse written in a late medieval manuscript
 Oxford, Bodleian Library, MS. Barlow 20 (f. 259v).
The University of Cambridge book curse
 Cambridge, Cambridge University Library Archives, UA Hare
 A.I, II (f. 4r).

A curse in a book of chemistry lectures
　　Cambridge, Gonville and Caius College, MS. 619/342 (flyleaf).
A Scots book curse written in an incunabulum
　　Cambridge, Cambridge University Library, Inc. 3. E. I. 4 [2787].
John Barclay's book curse, written in a medical book
　　Edinburgh, Royal College of Physicians, K 1.39.
A book curse with the name scratched out
　　San Marino CA, The Huntington Library, Rare Book 46130.
Jean Gemel's book curse
　　New York, New York Academy of Medicine, Gemel Book of
　　Recipes (p. 31).
Gerard Cooper's book curse
　　Baton Rouge, Louisiana State University, Rare Book Collection,
　　171 Er15a.
Mary Fearman's book curse, written in a book of fairy tales
　　Princeton NJ, University of Princeton, Cotsen Children's Library,
　　25143 English 18.
Elizabeth Parsons' book curse
　　Princeton NJ, University of Princeton, Cotsen Children's Library,
　　Eng 18 379.
Henry Pigot's book curse
　　Luton, University of Bedfordshire, Hockliffe Collection 0220.

MODERN BOOK CURSES

John Clare's book curse
　　Helpston, John Clare Cottage.
David H. Hooper's brain-beating book curse
　　Worcester MA, American Antiquarian Society, Dated Books.
Mary Lucretia Shelton's book curse
　　Worcester MA, American Antiquarian Society, Dated Books.
A Newgate Gaol book curse
　　Princeton NJ, University of Princeton, Cotsen Children's Library,
　　38349 Eng 18.